Crochet

PETITE FASHION ACCESSORIES

Crochet

PETITE FASHION ACCESSORIES

This edition published in 2012
By SpiceBox™
12171 Horseshoe Way
Richmond, BC
Canada V7A 4V4

First published in 2012
Copyright © SpiceBox™ 2012
All rights reserved.

ISBN 10: 1-77132-031-1
ISBN 13: 978-1-77132-031-3

CEO and Publisher: Ben Lotfi
Author: Cendrine Armani
Editorial: Ania Jaraczewski
Creative Director: Garett Chan
Art Director: Christine Covert
Design & Layout: Kirsten Reddecopp, Charmaine Muzyka
Production: James Badger, Mell D'Clute
Sourcing: Janny Lam
Photography: Remi Danzin, PepperMilk

For more SpiceBox products and information, visit our website:
www.spicebox.ca

Manufactured in China

1 3 5 7 9 10 8 6 4 2

Contents

The projects in this book are a wonderful introduction to the world of crafts.

Whether you're a beginner, or you have some experience, there will definitely be something here to keep you happy. Each project is illustrated by photographs or diagrams to guide you, and also contains detailed instructions. Once you've mastered the basics, let your imagination run wild as you make beautiful gifts for your nearest and dearest.

Tools & Materials

1 Yarn (various colors, thickness, types)

2 Thread (various colors)

3 Zippers

4 Crochet hooks (nos. 2.5 [2.25=B/1 and 2.75=C/2], 4[G/6], 8[L/11])

5 Metal keyrings

6 Clasps

7 Purse clasp (1 in [2.5 cm], 1.5 [4 cm])

8 Sequins (purple, green)

9 Paste gems

10 Seed beads ($1/16$ in [2 mm])

11 Sew-on cabochons

12 Metal hearts

13 Cover buttons (2.5 in [4 cm])

14 Paper balls

15 Wooden beads

16 Nylon thread (transparent)

17 Metal wallet clasp

Not pictured: Hand-sewing needles and extra-strong glue

Stitches - Skill Level: Beginner

Abbreviations

s	stitch
ch	chain stitch
sl st	slip stitch
sc	single crochet
hdc	half double crochet
dc	double crochet
tr	triple crochet
sc2tog	single crochet two together
dc2tog	double crochet two together
prev	previous
r	row
rep	repeat
tog	together

Repeat instructions inside
* * as indicated

Slip Knot

To start your crochet project, you first need to make a slip knot.

1 With your thumb, hold the yarn against the index and middle fingers of the same hand, with the tail end hanging down.

2 With the other hand, take the working yarn (the yarn closer to the ball, not the tail end) and wrap it around your index and middle fingers.

3 Still using the working yarn, bring a loop through the circle you've made around your fingers by pulling the yarn between your fingers from behind and in the direction your fingers are pointing.

4 Grasp the loop you've created in one hand, and the tail of the yarn in the other, and pull to tighten the knot. You should have an adjustable loop.

5 Slide your crochet hook into the loop and tighten it around the hook. You are now ready to begin crocheting.

Holding Your Crochet Hook and Yarn

1 Once you have placed a slip knot on your crochet hook, hold the hook in your dominant hand, as you would hold a pencil.

2 With the other hand, hold the tail end of the yarn close to the hook by grasping it with your thumb and middle finger.

3 Drape the working yarn over your index finger and hold it in your palm with your ring and middle fingers.

Chain Stitch (ch)

1 Bring the yarn that sits between your hook and your index finger over the hook from back to front. This is called a yarn over (yo). Turn the hook so that it grasps the yarn and pull the yarn through the loop on the hook. You have just made 1 chain, and you will have 1 loop on your hook.

2 Continue in this way for as many chains as required. You have now created the foundation for your crochet project.

Slip Stitch (sl st)

1 Insert the crochet hook into the first chain from the hook.

2 Yarn over.

3 Grasp the yarn with the hook and pull it through both the chain stitch and the loop on the hook.

Single Crochet (sc)

1 Skip 1 chain stitch and insert the hook into the second chain from the hook.

2 Yarn over and pull up a new loop through the chain stitch, but don't pull the yarn through the stitch on the hook. You will now have 2 loops on the hook.

3 Yarn over again and pull the yarn through both loops on the hook.

4 Sc in each of the following stitches. At the end of the row, chain 1 (this will take the place of your first sc in the next row). Turn your work so that you are now working into the stitches you made in the previous row.

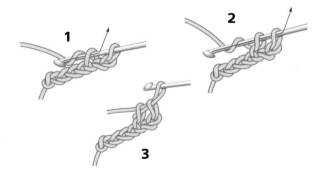

Half Double Crochet (hdc)

1 Yarn over and, without losing the loop created, insert the hook into the third chain from the hook.

2 Yarn over again and pull the yarn through the chain stitch, but do not pull it through the loop on the hook (3 loops on hook).

3 Yarn over for a third time and pull the yarn through all 3 loops on the hook.

4 You will now have 1 loop on the hook.

5 Hdc in each of the following stitches. At the end of the row, chain 2. Turn your work so that you are now working into the stitches you made in the previous row.

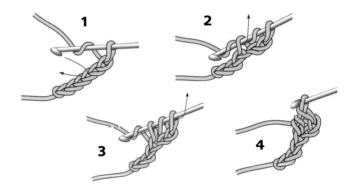

Double Crochet (dc)

1 Yarn over and insert the hook into the fourth chain from the hook.

2 Yarn over and pull the yarn through the stitch, but do not pull it through the loop on the hook (3 loops on hook).

3 Yarn over and pull the yarn through the first 2 loops on the hook (2 loops on hook).

4 Yarn over and pull the yarn through both loops on the hook

5 You will now have 1 loop on the hook.

6 Dc in each of the following stitches. At the end of the row, chain 3. Turn your work so that you are now working into the stitches you made in the previous row.

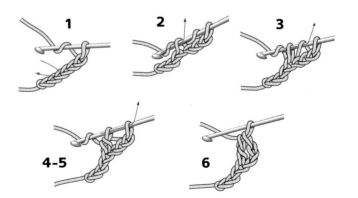

Triple/Treble Crochet (tr)

1 Yarn over twice and insert the hook into the fifth chain from the hook.

2 Yarn over again and pull the yarn through the chain stitch (4 loops on hook).

3 Yarn over again and pull the yarn through the first 2 loops (3 loops on hook).

4 Yarn over again and pull the yarn through 2 loops (2 loops on hook).

5 Yarn over again and pull the yarn through the 2 remaining loops.

6 You will now have 1 loop on your hook.

7 At the end of the row, chain 4. Turn your work so that you are now working into the stitches you made in the previous row.

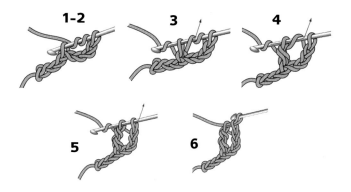

Single Crochet Two Together (sc2tog)

This method is used to decrease the number of stitches in a row.

1 Insert hook in next stitch, yarn over and pull the loop through the stitch (2 loops on hook).

2 Insert hook into next stitch, yarn over and pull the loop through the stitch (3 loops on hook).

3 Yarn over and pull the loop through all 3 loops on the hook at once (1 loop on hook).

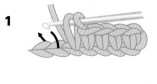

Double Crochet
Two Together (dc2tog)

1 Yarn over and insert the crochet hook into a stitch.

2 Yarn over again and pull the loop through the stitch.

3 Yarn over for a third time, bringing the yarn through the first 2 stitches on the crochet hook (this will give you an open double crochet).

4 Yarn over again and insert the crochet hook into the next stitch

5 Yarn over for a fifth time and pull the loop through the stitch.

6 Yarn over again and bring the yarn through the first 2 stitches (this will give you another open double crochet).

7 Yarn over again and bring the yarn through the 3 stitches. This will close up the 2 double crochets.

Fastening Off

At the end of your crochet piece, cut the yarn a few inches from your hook and pull the end of the yarn through the last loop on the hook. Pull the knot tight to secure. Weave the yarn tail into the fabric with a yarn needle.

Changing Yarn or Color

If you have reached the end of your ball of yarn, or want to change to a different color, use this method: Work the last stitch with the old yarn until just before the last step of the stitch. Hook the new yarn and pull it through the remaining loops on the hook, then continue working with the new yarn. For example, for single crochet, you would insert the hook into the next stitch and pull up a loop, hook the new yarn and pull the yarn through the 2 loops on the hook. Weave the ends of the yarn into the fabric with a yarn needle.

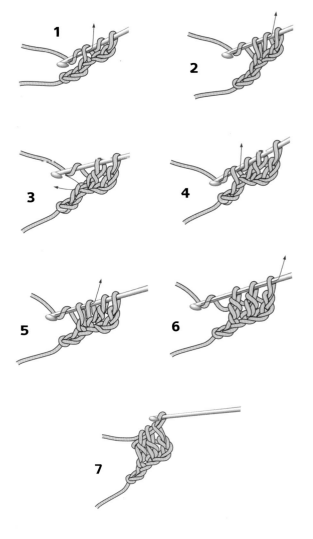

Crab Stitch

1 Make a foundation chain with any number of chain stitches. Make a row of single crochets. Chain 1.

2 Without turning your work, insert the hook into the first stitch from the hook from front to back, yarn over and pull the loop through.

3 Yarn over and pull the yarn through both stitches on the hook. Continue in this way to end of row.

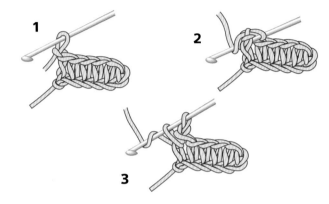

Russian Stitch

This stitch is made up of single crochets worked in the round so that every row is a right side row. Simply make every stitch a single crochet for as many rows as required.

Rose Stitch

This stitch is made up of rows of single crochets worked in both directions. At the end of each row, ch 1 before turning and beginning the next row of single crochets.

Rib Stitch

Usually when crocheting, you insert your hook through both top loops (strands) of the stitch in the previous row that you are working into. With rib stitch, you insert the hook into the back loop (the one farthest from you) only. After inserting your hook into the back loop, continue as you would normally with a single crochet stitch.

Granite Stitch

This stitch is made up of single crochets alternating with chain stitch. Make 1 ch (for 1 sc), 1 sc in the following s, *l ch, skip 1 s, 1 sc in the following s*. Repeat from * to * until you complete a row. For the following rows, insert the crochet hook under the ch of the previous rows.

Raised Stitch

Also known as "post stitch," this stitch is made by working around the posts (vertical shafts) of the stitch in the previous row, rather than the top loops. Insert the hook under the top 2 loops of the next stitch, as you would with a regular single crochet, then insert the hook under the top loops of the next stitch, from the back of the piece to the front. Yarn over and pull up a loop. Yarn over again and pull the loop through the 2 loops on the hook. Sc in next stitch. Continue the row, alternating between raised stitch and single crochet. Make a row of single crochets between each row of raised stitch.

Griddle Stitch

Make 3 ch (for 1 dc), then *2 ch, skip 2 s, 1 dc in the next s*. Repeat from * to * until you have completed the row. For the next rows, make 3 ch (for 1 dc) then *2 ch, 1 dc in the next dc*. Repeat from * to * until you have completed the row.

Mesh Stitch

This is worked on one side only and is used for round pieces of crochet. It is made up of arches of chain stitch. Make 1 ch (for 1 sc), *3 ch, skip 2 s, 1 sc in the next s*. Repeat from * to * until you have completed the round. To join, slip stitch in the 1st chain of the previous round. Sl st in next 2 s. Make 1 ch (for 1 sc), 3 ch, 1 sc in the middle of the first arch, *3 ch, 1 sc in the middle of the following arch*. Repeat from * to * until you have completed the round.

Fan Stitch

This stich is worked on one side only and is used for round pieces of crochet. It is made up of groups of dc separated by 1 sc. For the first round, make 1 ch (for the first sc), *skip 2 s, 5 dc in the next s. Skip 2 s, 1 sc in the next s*. Repeat from * to * until you have completed the round. Finish the round with 1 sl st in the first ch from the beginning of the round. For the next round, begin with 3 ch (for 1 dc), 2 dc by inserting the crochet hook in the ch, *1 sc in the third dc of the 5 dc group, 5 dc in the sc of the previous round*. Repeat from * to * until you have completed the round. Finish with 2 dc. Complete the round with 1 sl st in the third ch of the beginning of the round.

Wave Stitch

Chain 74. 1st row: Ch 3 (counts as 1st dc), dc in 4th chain from hook, dc in next 3 st, *make 5 dc in next st, dc in next 5 st, skip 2, 1 dc, skip 2*, rep from * to * 3 times, dc in next 5 st, 5 dc in next st, dc in next 5 st. 2nd row: Slip 2, ch 3 (counts as 1st dc), dc in next 4 st, *make 5 dc in next st, dc in next 5 st, skip 2, 1 dc, skip 2*, rep from * to * 3 times, dc in next 5 st, 5 dc in next st, dc in next 5 st. Rep row 2 until desired height achieved.

Popcorn Stitch

Popcorn stitch is worked on one side only and is used for round pieces of crochet. It is made up of single crochets and clusters of dc. To make the clusters, refer to the instructions for dc2tog (see page 10), but make a group of 6 dc this way, keeping the last loop from each dc on your hook until you have 7 loops on the hook. Yarn over and pull the yarn through all 7 loops at once. 1st round: 1 sc, *dc6tog, 3 sc*. Rep from * to * until you have completed the round. Crochet 3 rounds of sc. Rep from 1st round for as many rounds as required.

How to Make a Ball

Ch 5 and create a circle by making a sl st in the first chain.

1st round: Work 9 sc directly into the circle (not into the ch stitches). Sl st in first st.

2nd round: 2 sc in each s from the previous round. Sl st in first st. You should have 18 s.

3rd–9th rounds: 1 sc in each s from the previous round. Sl st in first st.

9th round: Insert a wooden bead or paper ball (as required).

10th–12th rounds: *Sc2tog. Rep from * till end of round.

How to Make a Flower

Chain 6 and create a circle by making a sl st in the first ch.

1st round: Working into the circle, 3 ch (for 1 dc), 2 ch, *1 dc, 2 ch*. Repeat 4 times from * to *. Finish with 1 sl st, inserting the crochet hook in the third ch from the beginning of the round.

2nd round: Work 1 ch (for 1 sc), 3 dc and 1 sc in the first arc of 2 ch, *Work 1 sc, 3 dc, 1 sc in the following arc*. Repeat 4 times from * to *. Finish with 1 sl st, inserting the crochet hook in the ch from the beginning of the round.

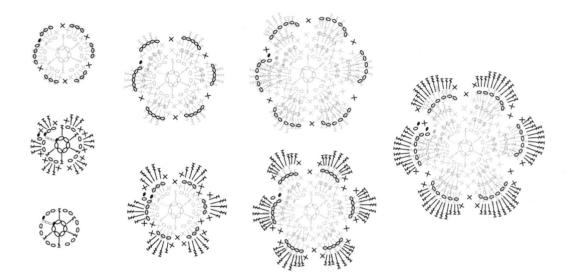

3rd round: 4 ch, *1 sc, inserting the crochet hook between the last sc of the last petal and the first sc of the next petal, 3 ch*. Repeat 4 times from * to *. Finish with 1 sl st, inserting the crochet hook in the first ch from the beginning of the round.

4th round: Work 1 ch (for 1 sc), 1 dc, 3 tr, 1 dc and 1 sc in the first arc, *Work 1 sc, 1 dc, 3 tr, 1 dc and 1 sc in the next arc*. Repeat 4 times from * to *. Finish with 1 sl st, inserting the crochet hook in the ch from the beginning of the round.

5th round: 6 ch, *I sc, inserting the crochet hook between the last sc of the last petal and the first sc of the next petal, 5 ch*. Repeat 4 times from * to *. Finish with 1 sl st, inserting the crochet hook in the first ch from the beginning of the round.

6th round: Work 1 ch (for 1 sc), 3 dc, 3 tr, 3 dc and 1 sc in the first arc. *Work 1 sc, 3 dc, 3 tr, 3 dc and 1 sc in the next arc*. Repeat 4 times from * to *. Finish with 1 sl st, inserting the crochet hook in the first ch from the beginning of the round.

7th round: 7 ch, *1 sc, inserting the crochet hook between the last sc of the last petal and the first sc of the next petal, 6 ch*. Repeat 4 times from * to *. Finish with 1 sl st, inserting the crochet hook in the first ch from the beginning of the round.

8th round: Work 1 ch (for 1 sc), 3 dc, 6 tr, 3 dc and 1 sc in the first arc, *Work 1 sc, 3 dc, 6 tr,, 3 dc and 1 sc in the next arc*. Repeat 4 times from * to *. Finish with 1 sl st, inserting the crochet hook in the ch from the beginning of the round. Fasten off.

Rainbows - Skill Level: Beginner

Materials
- 100% cotton yarn ($1/3$ oz [10 g] yellow, $1/3$ oz [10 g] red, $3/4$ oz [20 g] blue, 1 oz [25 g] orange, 1 $1/4$ oz [35 g] turquoise)
- No. 4 crochet hook
- Large needle

1. Red Cell Phone Pouch: Using the red yarn, chain 12. Make 1 row of sc. Make another row of sc, working into the back loops of the foundation chain. This will give you a round of 24 s. 2nd–13th round: Work rounds in mesh stitch (see page 14). Fasten off. To make the cord, chain 180, then work a row of sl st into the chain. Fasten off. Thread the cord you have just made between the arcs of the last round of the pouch, and sew the ends together.

2. Yellow Cell Phone Pouch: Using the red pouch instructions as a guide, make a pouch in yellow, making 15 rounds of mesh stitch. Fasten off. To make one cord, chain 40 and work a row of sl st into the chain. Fasten off. Make a second cord in the same way and thread the cords between the arcs of the last round of the pouch. Sew the ends together. Pull on the cords from either side to close the pouch.

3. Purse: Using the turquoise yarn, chain 28. Make 1 row of sc. Make another row of sc, working into the back loops of the foundation chain. This will give you a round of 56 s. 2nd–26th round: Work rounds in mesh stitch (see page 14). Fasten off. To make one cord, chain 80 and work a row of sl st into the chain. Fasten off. Make a second cord in the same way and thread the cords between the arcs of the last round of the purse. Sew the ends together. Pull on the cords from either side to close the pouch.

4. Sunglasses Case: Using the orange yarn, chain 12. Make 1 row of sc. Make another row of sc, working into the back loops of the foundation chain. This will give you a round of 24 s. 1st–32nd round: Work rounds in Russian stitch (see page 11). 33rd round: Make round in mesh stitch (see page 14), skipping 1 s instead of 2. Fasten off. To make the cord, chain 50 and work 1 row of sl st into the chain. Fasten off. Thread the cord you have just made between the arcs of the last round of the case and sew the ends together.

5. Wallet: Using the blue yarn, chain 14. Make 1 row of sc. Make another row of sc, working into the back loops of the foundation chain. This will give you a round of 28 s. 2nd–16th round: Work rounds in Russian stitch (see page 11). 17th round: Work round in mesh stitch (see page 14), skipping 1 s instead of 2. Fasten off. To make one cord, chain 45 and work 1 row of sl st into the chain. Fasten off. Make a second cord in the same way and thread them both between the arcs of the last round of the wallet. Sew the ends together. Pull on the cords from either side to close the wallet.

Moody Blue - Skill Level: Intermediate

1. Purse: Chain 48. Make 1 row of double crochet (see page 8). Make another row of dc, working into the back loops of the foundation chain. This will give you a round of 96 s. 2nd–21st round: Work rounds in double crochet. 22nd round: Make 1 round in griddle stitch (see page 13), crocheting 1 ch and skipping 1 s instead of 2. 23rd–25th round: Work in fan stitch (see page 14). 26th round: Work round in crab stitch (see page 11). Fasten off. To make cord, chain 120 and work 1 row of sl st into the chain. Fasten off. Make a second cord in the same way and thread them between the arcs made by the griddle stitch in the purse. Sew the ends together. Pull the cords from each side to close the purse.

2. Bracelet: Make 5 balls, following the instructions on page 16. Thread the elasticated thread through each ball, inserting a blue bead between each one. Knot the ends and cut off any excess thread.

3. Wallet: Chain 15. Make 1 row of granite stitch (see page 12). Make another row of granite stitch, working into the back loops of the foundation chain. This will give you a round of 30. 2nd–19th round: Work in granite stitch. 20th round: Work in crab stitch (see page 11). Fasten off. Sew on the zipper.

Materials

- DMC SENSO yarn no. 770 (blue no. 1705)
- No. 2.5 crochet hook
- 5 beads (3/4 in [2.2 cm] diameter, blue)
- 5 wooden beads (1 in [2.5 cm] diameter)
- Transparent elasticated thread
- 1 zipper (4 in [10 cm] long, purple)
- Large needle
- Hand-sewing needle
- Thread (purple)

Summer Fruits - Skill Level: Intermediate

Materials

- 100% cotton yarn (3 oz [90 g], white)
- DMC SENSO yarn no. 700 (yellow no. 1003, red no. 1006, fuchsia no. 1008, green no. 1009)
- DMC SENSO yarn no. 740 (white no. 1401)
- DMC SENSO yarn no. 730 (plum no. 1308)
- No. 2.5 crochet hook
- No. 4 crochet hook
- Large needle
- Pin (4 in [10 cm] long, gold-colored)
- 2 clasps (1 1/3 in [3.5 cm] long, silver)
- 2 keyrings (2/3 in [1.5 cm] diameter)
- Stuffing

1. Small Strawberry:
Using the red cotton yarn, chain 5. Sl st in 1st chain to make a circle. 1st round: Working into the circle, 1 ch (for 1 sc), 5 sc. 2nd round: 1 ch (for 1 sc), 1 sc, 2 sc in each of the next s. 3rd–8th round: 12 sc. Stuff the strawberry. 9th round: Sc2tog 6 times. 10th round: Using green yarn, sc2tog 3 times. Make 5 ch and 1 sl st on each ch stitch (to make the stalk). Cut yarn and pull through last loop on hook to fasten off. Weave in the green yarn with the needle. To make leaves, ch 5 and sl st in 1st ch to make a circle. Make 1 ch (for 1 sc), *4 ch, 1 ch (for 1 sc), 1 sc on each of the 4 ch, 1 sc*. Repeat from * to * 4 times. Fasten off. Attach the stalk in the middle of the leaves. To make seeds, embroider a few stitches in white yarn on the strawberry.

2. Large Strawberry:
Using the red yarn, chain 5 and sl st in the first ch to make a circle. 1st round: Working into the circle, make 1 ch (for 1 sc), 8 sc. 2nd–4th rounds: 9 sc. 5th round: 1 ch (for 1 sc), 1 sc, 2 sc in each of the following s. 6th–12th rounds: 18 sc. Stuff the strawberry. 13th round: sc2tog 9 times. 14th round: Switch to green yarn and continue to sc2tog around. To make the stalk, make 5 ch and 1 sl st in each ch. Fasten off and weave in ends. Make leaves and fix them to the large strawberry in the same way you did with the small strawberry.

3. Brooch & Keychain:
Following the instructions on page 16, make a flower, using yellow yarn for the first round and white yarn for the second round. Finish off your work after the second round and sew the flower to the pin. Make 1 large and 1 small strawberry. Sew them onto the pin for the brooch. Attach the fruit to the keyrings.

4. Watermelon Slice:
Using the fuchsia yarn, chain 5 and sl st in the first ch to make a circle. 1st round: Working into the circle, 1 ch (for 1 sc), 8 sc. 2nd–5th rounds: 1 ch (for 1 sc), *1 sc, 2 sc in the following s*. Repeat from * to * for the entire round. 6th round: You should have 48 s. Using the green yarn, make 1 sc in each of the 48 s. 7th round: Make *3 sl st, 3 sc, 3 hdc, 3 dc, 6 tr, 3 dc, 3 sc, 3 sl st*. Repeat once from * to *. Fold the work in half and stitch the back of the watermelon slice, leaving a gap for the stuffing. Close the gap after stuffing.

5. White Purse:
Using the white yarn and the no. 4 crochet hook, chain 36. Crochet a row of fan stitch (see page 14). Then work another row of fan stitch into the back loops of the foundation chain. You will have a round of 72 s. 2nd–14th round: Continue to work rounds in fan stitch. 15th round: Make a round in griddle stitch (see page 13), crocheting 1 sc in the third dc of each group of 5 dc, and 1 dc on each sc of the previous round. 16th–21st: Work in fan stitch. 22nd round: Work in crab stitch (see page 11). To make the cord, chain 100 and sl st into each ch. Fasten off. Make a second cord in the same way and thread them between the arcs made by the griddle stitch. Sew the ends together. Pull the cords from each side to close the purse. Make 2 small strawberries and a slice of watermelon and sew them to the front of the purse.

Pretty in Pink - Skill Level: Intermediate

Materials

- 100% cotton yarn (pink, brown, ecru, gray, mauve, red, fuchsia)
- No. 4 crochet hook
- No. 2.5 crochet hook
- 2 zippers (6 in [15 cm] long; 1 fuchsia, 1 gray)
- Large needle
- Hand-sewing needle
- Thread
- 3 pink cabochons

1. Pouch - Vertical Stripes: Using the pink yarn and the no. 4 crochet hook, chain 60. 1st–38th row: Work in rose stitch (see page 11) as follows: 1 row pink, 2 rows brown, 1 row ecru, 5 rows gray, 2 rows mauve, 1 row red, 2 rows fuchsia, 2 rows red, 3 rows brown, 6 rows ecru, 1 row pink, 1 row ecru, 4 rows gray, 1 row brown, 1 row red, 2 rows mauve, 1 row pink, 2 rows mauve. Fold the work in 2 and sew up the sides. Fold the top of the wallet over twice by 1 in (2.5 cm). Stitch the overlap in place and sew the ecru zipper into place.

2. Wallet: Using the DMC fuchsia yarn and no. 2.5 crochet hook, chain 5 and sl st in the first ch to make a circle. 1st round: Working into the circle, 3 ch (for 1 dc), 11 dc. 2nd and 3rd rounds: 3 ch (for 1 dc), 2 dc in each s of the previous row. 4th round: 3 ch (for 1 dc), 1 dc in each s of the previous row. 5th round: 3 ch (for 1 dc), 2 dc in each s of the previous row. 6th round: 1 ch (for 1 sc), 1 sc in each s of the previous row. Fasten off. Thread 75 sequins onto the fuchsia yarn. Make the second side of the wallet in the same way as you made the first, but this time add 1 sequin before you yarn on every third double crochet. Sew the sides together and sew on the 6 in (15 cm) zipper.

3. Pouch - Horizontal Stripes: Using the pink yarn and no. 4 crochet hook, chain 28. Make 1 row of sc. Make another row of sc, working into the back loops of the foundation chain. You will have a round of 56 s. 2nd–26th round: Work in raised stitch (see page 13), making stripes of 2 rounds each with the pink, mauve, ecru and fuchsia yarn. 27th round: Work in crab stitch (see page 11) with the mauve yarn. Fasten off. Sew on the 6 in (15 cm) fuchsia zipper.

4. Cabochon Purse: Using the gray yarn, chain 18 and crochet 44 rows in rose stitch (see page 11). This rectangle will be the back and flap of the purse. Chain 18 and crochet 30 rows in rose stitch. This rectangle will be the front of the purse. Chain 78 and crochet 5 rows in rose stitch. This will be the sides and bottom of the purse. Use sc to fix the sides to the front and back of the purse. Make a row of mauve sc to trim the purse. To make the cord, chain 150 and sl st in each ch. Fasten off. Sew the ends of the cord inside the purse and sew the pink cabochons on the flap.

Cocoa Crazy - Skill Level: Intermediate

1. Purse: Using the brown yarn and the no. 4 crochet hook, chain 30. Crochet 1 row of sc. Make another row of sc, working into the back loops of the foundation chain. You will have a round of 60 s. 2nd–40th round: Work in popcorn stitch (see page 15). 41st round: Work 1 round of sc in the mustard yarn. 42nd round: Work in crab stitch (see page 11) with the beige yarn. Fasten off. To make the cord, chain 175 using the brown yarn, and sl st into each chain. Fasten off. Sew the ends of the cord inside the purse.

2. Wallet: Using the straw-colored yarn and no. 4 crochet hook, chain 16. Crochet 1 row of sc. Crochet another row of sc, working into the back loops of the foundation chain. You will have a round of 32 s. 2nd–15th round: Work in popcorn stitch (see page 15). 16th round: Make a round of sc with the beige yarn. 17th round: Work in crab stitch (see page 11) with the mustard yarn. Fasten off. Sew on the zipper.

3. Bracelet: Make 5 balls with the beige DMC yarn and the no. 2.5 crochet hook. To make each ball, start with a foundation chain of 5 ch, joined into a circle. 1st round: Working into the circle, make 6 sc. 2nd round: 2 sc in each s of the preceding round. You will have 12 s. 3rd–6th rounds: 1 sc in each s of the preceding round. Insert a paper ball. 7th round: sc2tog 6 times. Fasten off and sew the center closed. Thread the crochet balls onto the transparent elasticated thread, alternating them with the beads. Knot the ends and cut off any excess thread.

Materials

- 100% cotton yarn (3 1/2 oz [110 g] brown, 1 1/4 oz [30 g] straw-colored, 1/3 oz [10 g] mustard, 1/3 oz [10 g] beige)
- DMC SENSO Metallics yarn no. 740 (beige no. 1402)
- No. 4 crochet hook
- No. 2.5 crochet hook
- 1 zipper (4 in [10 cm] long, beige)
- 6 paper balls (2/3 in [1.5 cm] diameter)
- 6 beads (1/3 in [1 cm] diameter, beige)
- Large needle
- Hand-sewing needle
- Thread (beige)
- Transparent elasticated thread (8 in [20 cm])

Blue Skies - Skill Level: Advanced

Materials

- 100% cotton yarn (3 oz [80 g] blue, 3 oz [80 g] sky blue)
- Fancy yarn
- No. 4 crochet hook
- No. 8 crochet hook
- Large needle
- Hand-sewing needle
- 1 sew-on paste gem (1.5 x 1 in [4 x 3 cm], transparent)
- 2 zippers (6 in [15 cm], sky blue)
- 2 metal hearts (1.5 in [4 cm] wide, silver)
- Thread (sky blue)

1. **Purse:** Using the sky blue yarn, chain 36. Make 1 row in granite stitch (see page 12). Make another row in granite stitch, working into the back loops of the foundation chain. You will have a round of 72 s. 2nd–30th round: Work in granite stitch, alternating rows between blue and sky blue yarn. 31st round: Make a round in griddle stitch (see page 13), crocheting 1 ch and skipping 1 s instead of 2. 32rd–38th round: With the blue yarn, work in granite stitch. 39th round: Make 1 round in griddle stitch. 40th round: Work in fan stitch (see page 14), inserting the crochet hook in each of the arcs formed by the griddle stitch. Fasten off. To make the cord, chain 150 and sl st into each chain s. Fasten off. Thread the cord between the arcs made by the griddle stitch (31st round) and attach a heart shape to each end, sewing the ends to keep the hearts in place. Pull the cord from each side to gather the purse and knot them in front.

2. **Gem Clutch:** Using the blue yarn, chain 30. Make a row in fan stitch (see page 14). Make another row in fan stitch, working into the back loops of the foundation chain. You will have a round of 60s. 2nd–13th round: Work in fan stitch, alternating each round between blue and sky blue yarn. 14th round: Work in crab stitch (see page 11) with the blue yarn. Fasten off. Sew the zipper onto the clutch, and sew the paste gem to the front.

3. **Fantasy Clutch:** Using the fancy yarn and no. 8 crochet hook, chain 12. Make a row in Russian stitch (see page 11). Make another row in Russian stitch, working into the back loops of the foundation chain. You will have a round of 24 s. 2nd–10th round: Work in Russian stitch. Fasten off. Turn your work over (the fancy yarn will look thicker). 11th round: Using the sky blue yarn and no. 4 crochet hook, insert the crochet hook in 1 stitch of the last round of fancy yarn and make 1 sc, *1 ch, 1 sc in the next stitch*. Repeat from * to * for the entire round. 12th round: Make a round of sc, inserting the crochet hook in each sc and ch of the previous round. 13th–15th round: Make 1 round of sc in sky blue, then 1 round in blue, then another round in sky blue. 16th round: Finish with a round of crab stitch (see page 11) in blue. Fasten off and sew on the zipper.

Beach Babes - Skill Level: Advanced

Materials

- 100% cotton yarn (1 ¼ oz [30 g] yellow, 1 ½ oz [40 g] maroon, $\frac{1}{3}$ oz [10 g] orange, 1 oz [35 g] mauve, 1 oz [35 g] fuchsia)
- No. 4 crochet hook
- 2 sew-on paste gems (1.5 x 1 in [4 x 3 cm]; 1 pink, 1 yellow)
- 2 zippers (one 4 in [10 cm] long, one 6 in [15 cm] long, both maroon)
- 1 large needle
- 1 hand-sewing needle
- Thread (maroon)

1. Clutch: With the mauve yarn, chain 24. Crochet a row of sc. Crochet another row of sc into the back loops of the foundation chain. This will give you a round of 48 s. Work in Russian stitch (see page 11) as follows: 1 row mauve, 1 row fuchsia, 1 row maroon, 2 rows fuchsia, 2 rows mauve, 1 row yellow, 1 row orange, 1 row yellow, 1 row fuchsia, 4 rows mauve, 1 row fuchsia, 1 row maroon, 2 rows fuchsia, 1 row mauve. Make a row in crab stitch (see page 11) with the mauve yarn. Fasten off. Sew the pink paste gem and the 6 in [15 cm] zipper on the clutch. Sew the ends of the cord together inside the pouch.

2. Purse: With the maroon yarn, chain 28. Crochet a row of sc. Crochet another row of sc, working into the back loops of the foundation chain. This will give you a round of 56. Work in Russian stitch (see page 11) as follows: 1 row maroon, 1 row fuchsia, 1 row orange, 2 rows fuchsia, 2 rows maroon, 1 row mauve, 1 row yellow, 1 row mauve, 1 row fuchsia, 4 rows maroon, 1 row fuchsia, 1 row orange, 2 rows fuchsia, 2 rows maroon, 1 row mauve, 1 row yellow, 1 row mauve, 1 row fuchsia, 4 rows maroon, 1 row fuchsia, 1 row orange, 2 rows fuchsia, 2 rows maroon. Make a row in crab stitch (page 11) with the maroon yarn. Fasten off. Using the maroon yarn again, chain 150 and sl st into each chain s. Fasten off and sew the ends of the cord together inside the purse. Sew the yellow paste gem on the front.

3. Wallet: With the maroon yarn, chain 18. Crochet a row of sc. Crochet another row of sc, working into the back loops of the foundation chain. This will give you a round of 36. Work in Russian stitch (see page 11) as follows: 1 row maroon, 1 row fuchsia, 1 row orange, 2 rows fuchsia, 2 rows maroon, 1 row mauve, 1 row yellow, 1 row mauve, 1 row fuchsia, 2 rows maroon. Make a row in crab stitch (see page 11) with the maroon yarn. Fasten off and sew on the 4 in [10 cm] zipper.

4. Cell Phone Pouch: With the yellow yarn, chain 12. Crochet a row of sc. Crochet another row of sc, working into the back loops of the foundation chain. This will give you a round of 24. Work in Russian stitch (see page 11) as follows: 1 row yellow, 1 row fuchsia, 1 row mauve, 2 rows fuchsia, 2 rows yellow, 1 row orange, 1 row maroon, 1 row orange, 1 row fuchsia, 4 rows yellow, 1 row fuchsia, 1 row mauve, 2 rows fuchsia, 2 rows yellow. Make a row in crab stitch (see page 11) with the yellow yarn. Fasten off. Using the yellow yarn again, chain 150 and sl st into each ch. Fasten off and sew the ends of the cord together inside the pouch.

Chill - Skill Level: Advanced

Materials

- 100% cotton yarn (1 3/4 oz [50 g] beige, 1 3/4 oz [50 g] ecru)
- No. 4 crochet hook
- 1 zipper (4 in [10 cm] long, beige)
- 1 clasp (1 1/3 in [3.5 cm], antique gold)
- 2 clasps (1 in [2.3 cm] long, antique gold)
- Large needle
- Hand-sewing needle
- Thread (beige)

1. Eyeglass Case: Using the ecru yarn and the no. 4 crochet hook, chain 12. Make a row in granite stitch (see page 12). Make another row in granite stitch, working into the back loops of the foundation chain. This will give you a round of 24 s. 2nd–34th round: Work in granite stitch, alternating every other row between ecru and beige. 35th round: Use the ecru yarn to make a row in fan stitch (see page 14). Fasten off. Make a strap by making a chain of 14 ch and making a sl st in each ch. Fasten off. Attach the clasp to one end of the strap and sew the other end of the strap to the back of the case. Make a second strap in the same way. Attach the lock of the clasp to the front of the case.

2. Wallet: Using the ecru yarn and the no. 4 crochet hook, chain 18. Make a row in granite stitch (see page 12). Make another row in granite stitch, working into the back loops of the foundation chain. This will give you a round of 32 s. 2nd–13th round: Work in granite stitch, alternating every other row between ecru and beige. 14th round: Make a final round in fan stitch (see page 14) with the beige yarn. Fasten off and sew on the zipper.

3. Cell Phone Pouch: Using the ecru yarn and the no. 4 crochet hook, chain 14. Make a row in granite stitch (see page 12). Make another row in granite stitch, working into the back loops of the foundation chain. This will give you a round of 28 s. 2nd–23rd round: Work in granite stitch, alternating each row between ecru and beige. 24th round: Make a final round in fan stitch (see page 14) with the beige yarn. Fasten off. To make the strap, chain 16, then make 1 row of sc, and another row of sc in the back loops of the foundation chain. Fasten off. Attach the clasp to one end of the strap and sew the other end of the strap to the back of the pouch. Attach the lock of the clasp to the front of the pouch. To make the cord, chain 150 with the beige yarn and sl st into each ch. Fasten off and sew the ends of the strap to the inside of the pouch.

Dream of the Andes - *Skill Level: Advanced*

Materials

- 100% cotton yarn (beige, ecru, red, maroon, sky blue, yellow, fuchsia, khaki)
- No. 4 crochet hook
- 4 plastic bracelets
- 1 large needle

1. Purse: Using the khaki yarn, chain 72. 2nd–27th row: Work in rose stitch (see page 11) as follows: 1 row khaki, 1 row sky blue, 1 row maroon, 3 rows ecru, 2 rows maroon, 2 rows yellow, 2 rows beige, 1 row fuchsia, 3 rows beige, 2 rows sky blue, 3 rows khaki, 1 row ecru, 1 row maroon, 2 rows red, 1 row maroon, 1 row khaki. Fold the crocheted work over by 26 rows and attach the sides with a row of sc in khaki yarn. Trim the flap with a row of fan stitch (see page 14). To make the cord, chain 150 and sl st in each ch. Fasten off and sew the ends of the strap to the inside of the purse.

2. Bracelets: Chain 32 and join into a circle with 1 sl st in the first ch. 2nd–12th round: Work in Russian stitch (see page 11) as follows:

Bracelet A: 5 rows ecru, 1 row maroon, 2 rows red, 1 row maroon, 3 rows ecru

Bracelet B: 5 rows khaki, 2 rows sky blue, 3 rows beige, 2 rows khaki

Bracelet C: 5 rows beige, 2 rows yellow, 1 row beige, 1 row fuchsia, 3 rows beige

Bracelet D: 5 rows khaki, 1 row maroon, 2 rows red, 1 row maroon, 3 rows khaki

Sew each crocheted band around a plastic bracelet.

Sunshine Flowers - Skill Level: Advanced

Materials

- 100% cotton yarn (2 oz [60 g], beige)
- DMC SENSO yarn no. 700 (bright yellow no. 1003)
- DMC SENSO yarn no. 710 (pale yellow no. 1102)
- DMC SENSO yarn no. 720 (beige no. 1202)
- No. 4 crochet hook
- No. 2.5 crochet hook
- 1 zipper (4 $\frac{3}{4}$ in [12 cm] long, beige)
- 21 sew-on paste gems ($\frac{2}{16}$ in [6 mm] diameter, yellow)
- 5 stick-on paste gems ($\frac{3}{16}$ in [4 mm] diameter; 2 purple, 2 yellow, 1 red)
- 1 clasp (1 $\frac{1}{2}$ in [4 cm] long, antique gold)
- Large needle
- Hand-sewing needle
- Thread (beige)

1. Purse: Using the beige yarn and the no. 4 crochet hook, chain 22. Make a row of sc. Make another row of sc, working into the back loops of the foundation chain. This will give you a round of 44 s. 2nd–32nd round: Work in Russian stitch (see page 11). 33rd round: Work in crab stitch (see page 11). Fasten off. To make strap, chain 200 and sl st in each ch. Fasten off and sew the ends of this strap inside the purse. Sew a flower on the front of the purse (see photograph.)

2. Flowers: Using the bright yellow yarn and no. 2.5 crochet hook, make 3 flowers. For each one, chain 5 and join in a circle with 1 sl st in the first ch. Crochet 1 ch (for 1 sc) then *6 ch, 3 ch (for 1 dc), 1 dc on each of the 6 ch, 1 sc by inserting the crochet hook into the circle*. Repeat from * to * 5 times. Make 1 sl st in the first ch at the start of the round, then fasten off. Sew 7 gems in the center of each flower.

3. Wallet: Using the pale yellow yarn and no. 2.5 crochet hook, chain 31. 2nd–9th row: Using the bright yellow yarn, work in griddle stitch (see page 13). 10th row: Make a row of sc, crocheting 3 sc in each arc. 11th row: Sc in each s. Make 1 row of sc around the edges of the piece of fabric. To make the back of the wallet, chain 30 using the beige yarn and no 2.5 crochet hook. Crochet 8 rows in double crochet (see page 8) then 3 rows in sc. Sew the two sides together and sew on the zipper. Sew 2 flowers onto the griddle stitch.

4. Key Chain:

Head: Using the beige DMC yarn and the no. 2.5 crochet hook, make a ball (see page 16).

Body: Using the bright yellow, make a ball in rib stitch (see page 12).

Skirt: Make a round of *1 sc, 2 sc in the next s*, inserting the crochet hook in the strands of the 3rd round of the yellow ball, and crochet 4 rounds in rib stitch. Trim this with a row of fan stitch (see page 14) in pale yellow yarn. Fasten off.

Arms: Chain 9 with the beige yarn, then 3 ch (for 1 dc), 4 dc by inserting the crochet hook in the same stitch and 1 sl st on each of the remaining 8 s. Repeat to make the second arm.

Hat: Follow the instructions on how to make a ball and make one using rib stitch to the 7th round. Trim with crab stitch (see page 11) in pale yellow yarn. Fasten off.

Assembly: Using the beige yarn, chain 6. Thread the chain onto the keyring and through the hat and sew it to the head. Sew on the arms and body. Glue on gems for the eyes, mouth and buttons (see photograph).

Shades of Evening - Skill Level: Advanced

Materials

- DMC SENSO yarn no. 730 (mauve no. 1307, maroon no. 1308, green no. 1304)
- DMC SENSO yarn no. 720 (pink no. 1205)
- No. 2.5 crochet hook
- 1 zipper (4 3/4 in [12 cm] long, green)
- 26 sequins (4/16 in [6 mm] diameter, purple, green)
- 26 seed beads (1/16 in [2 mm] diameter, pink)
- 1 cover button (1.5 in [4 cm] diameter)
- 1 cabochon (3/4 in x 1/2 in [2 x 1.5 cm], purple)
- 1 wallet clasp (3 in [8 cm] wide, antique gold)
- 1 brooch frame
- Large needle
- Hand-sewing needle
- Thread (beige)
- Extra-strong glue

1. Wallet: Using the mauve yarn, chain 24. Make 1 row of dc (see page 8). Make a second row of dc by working into the back loops of the foundation chain. You will have a round of 48 s. 2nd–7th round: Work rounds in double crochet rib stitch (see page 12, but use dc instead of sc). 8th–9th round: Work in Russian stitch (see page 11). Fasten off. Crochet the pleats in Russian stitch with the mauve yarn by inserting the crochet hook below the strands (created by the rib stitch) of the 2nd, 4th and 6th rounds. Crochet 1 round in sc. Crochet *1 sc, 2 sc in the next s* to make a second round. Repeat from * to * on the whole round. Make 2 rounds of sc and finish with a round of crab stitch (see page 11) in maroon yarn. Make the two other pleats in the same way. Using the pink yarn, crochet 8 rows in rose stitch (see page 11) on the center 8 s of each side. Fasten off. To attach the clasp, place a few drops of glue on the metal parts of the clasp. Gently put it in place on the pink crochet. Sew the cabochon to the front of the wallet.

2. Clutch: Using the green yarn, make a chain of 60 ch and work in wave stitch (see page 14) for 13 rows, changing color each row. Fold the rectangle in half, sew the sides together and sew on the zipper.

3. Decorative Button: Using the pink yarn, make a chain of 5 ch and fix it in a circle with 1 sl st in the first ch. 1st round: 6 sc, inserting the crochet hook in the round. 2nd round: 2 sc in each s of the previous round. You will have 12 s. 3rd round: 2 sc in each s of the previous round. You will have 24 s. 4th round: Using the green yarn, make 1 sc in each s of the previous round. 5th round: Using the maroon yarn, make 1 sc in each s of the previous round. 6th round: Using the mauve yarn, make 1 sc in each s of the previous round. Sew the sequins and gems in the center of the clutch. Cover the button and sew it on the front of the clutch.

4. Flowered Brooch: Follow the directions on page 16 to make the flower. Crochet the first 3 rounds in mauve, the next 2 in maroon, the next 2 in green and the last in pink. Sew the beads and sequins in the center of the flower and attach the brooch frame to the back.